TEMPTATIONS

Rev. P. J. Michel, S.J.

TEMPTATIONS

Where They Come From, What They Mean, and How to Defeat Them

Translated from the French by
Rev. F. P. Garesché, S.J.

SOPHIA INSTITUTE PRESS
Manchester, New Hampshire

These pages are excerpted from Fr. Michel's larger 1904 work, *Spiritual Despondency and Temptations* (New York: Benziger Brothers), and include minor editorial revisions.

Printed in the United States of America.

Cover and interior design by Perceptions Design Studio.

On the cover: *The Torments of Hell* (fresco), by Joseph Anton Koch (1768–1839) / Casino Massimo, Rome, Italy / Bridgeman Images.

Except where otherwise noted, Scripture passages are taken from the Douay-Rheims edition of the Old and New Testaments. Where applicable, quotations have been cross-referenced with the differing names and enumeration in the Revised Standard Version, using the following symbol: [RSV =].

Nihil obstat: Remigius LaFort, S.T.L., *Censor*

Imprimatur: John M. Farley
Archbishop of New York
New York, January 2, 1904

Sophia Institute Press
Box 5284, Manchester, NH 03108
1-800-888-9344

www.SophiaInstitute.com

Sophia Institute Press® is a registered trademark of Sophia Institute.

Library of Congress Cataloging-in-Publication Data
TK

First printing

CONTENTS

TEMPTATIONS

CHAPTER 1

Temptations Are Not Proof of God's Having Abandoned Us

Temptations trouble pious souls and plunge the dissipated over the precipice. In order to prevent the evil that temptations may produce, it is well to give you the reasons for not fearing them, the principles by which you should be guided on different occasions, the way in which you should behave when assailed and by which you may preserve yourself against their assaults, and, finally, the advantages you may derive from them.

A temptation is a thought, a feeling, an inclination, or a tendency that solicits us to violate the law of God for our own satisfaction. A temptation should neither trouble nor discourage a Christian soul.

The devil declares war especially against those who detest his rule, who fight against their passions, who are disciples of Jesus Christ as much by their purity of love as by the ineffaceable seal of regeneration, or against those who seriously think of throwing off the yoke that he has imposed upon them. In his attempts against them, he seeks only to make them renounce the love of Jesus Christ, to separate them from God by making them his partners in disobedience.

This reflection should be the consolation of those who are tempted. It is their contradiction with him, the enemy of their salvation, their love for piety and for the will of God, that draws upon them this persecution. A little perseverance will make them victorious and, above all, will strengthen them in virtue.

Souls who are naturally timid, or whom the Lord has conducted for a long time by a cessation of passion and the sweetness of peace, are apt to imagine that these temptations they sometimes experience are signs of God's anger, and they even come to think themselves abandoned when the temptation becomes strong and frequent. They cannot persuade themselves that God can look with a favorable eye upon a heart agitated by sentiments so opposed to virtue.

This is the last resource of the enemy for the overthrow of a soul that he has been unable to seduce by the empty pleasures of vice. He takes away that precious confidence that would sustain it against all the assaults of hell.

Such souls are greatly deceived. Those who are instructed, who are better acquainted with the ways of providence, are not surprised at the struggle in which they are engaged. They have learned from the Holy Spirit that the life of man is a perpetual combat; that we are obliged to defend ourselves, without ceasing, from within, against our tastes, our inclinations, our self-love, domestic enemies who are ever ready to betray us by their snares and their suggestions; from without, against the influence of bad example, human respect, and the powers of hell, jealous of man's happiness and conspiring against him from the beginning of the world.

They know that it is only by the victories that we gain through the assistance of grace that we force our way to heaven, and that, according to the apostle, "He also that striveth for the mastery is not crowned except he strive lawfully" (2 Tim. 2:5).

St. Paul, although he prayed to be delivered from them, did not regard the temptations that he continued to experience as signs of God's having abandoned him. The saints, so long and so violently attacked by the devil, even in the desert and in the exercise of the severest penance, also had not this idea of temptations. On the contrary, they always regarded temptations as the object of their struggles and the subject of their merit. They knew what was said in the Holy Scripture: "Because thou wast acceptable to God, it was necessary that temptation should prove thee" (Tob. 12:13).

This is the view that you too should take—it is the only one that is correct according to the principles of religion—and then you will no longer be troubled or discouraged.

But, although temptations are no sign of our being forsaken—since God never entirely abandons man as long as he is alive—and although they are generally a trial of the just, yet they are sometimes the effect of divine justice, which punishes thereby our negligence in the divine service, the weakness of slothful and presumptuous souls, and the indulgence of natural inclinations.

But whether they be a punishment or a trial, our submission in receiving them and our fidelity in resisting them must be still the same. From the most loving of Fathers we cannot expect a justice unaccompanied by mercy. His grace always follows on prayer and confidence. He does not desire our destruction; He punishes us only to regain us. And so far from being discouraged and troubled, we should be animated in the combat by the pardon that is extended to us, if, with a humble and contrite heart, we faithfully perform the penance that God imposes.

CHAPTER 2

Temptations Are Not a Sign of a Dangerous State of Soul

Frequent temptations may prove that the heart is subject to passions and inclined to evil, but, when rejected, they do not indicate that it is bad or separated from God. This inclination to evil that we inherit as a consequence of the sin of our first parents is sometimes increased by the influence of the senses on the soul. They render us more or less subject to temptation, according as their impressions are more or less strong, and this, being independent of our will and not having its origin in the heart, does not indicate a vicious state. It is not the cause of this sensible disturbance; on the contrary, it suffers from it; and when from its love for virtue it corrects the inclination, strong as it may be, the heart certainly does not become the worse for the effort.

This resistance to temptation shows a Christian heart, displays its attachment to God and the protection that He affords it, and is a source of con-solation and confidence. This resolution to resist the inclination that solicits it comes from the divine goodness that furnishes it with graces all the more powerful in proportion to its danger.

It is poor reasoning to say: if my mind and heart were in a good condition and well with God, should I have these thoughts and feelings so opposed to faith, to submission, to patience, which cause me such horror?

If these thoughts and feelings depended solely on your will—to have them or not—you might, with some show of reason, deem yourself at enmity with God when you recognize their presence. But it does not depend wholly on you. These thoughts and feel-ings insinuate themselves silently, or violently possess themselves of your mind and heart without consulting your will, and what is more, they endure in spite of your will, which would free itself of them and uses every means for their expulsion. They are not, there-fore, the result of your free will; they are not of your choosing; and they can decide nothing concerning the good state of your soul, or against its union with God and virtue.

The heart becomes attached to an object only through deliberation and voluntary action. It can, therefore, belong to God even though it is exposed to involuntary feelings that are contrary to virtue and which it condemns.

I may say more; the pain that it feels and the horror that it conceives at being thus assailed are a decisive proof that it is faithful to its duty and to divine love. If it loved God less, if it feared and hated sin less, it would not experience this pain, and trouble, and horror; it would listen to its inclinations and satisfy its desires. It cannot have any surer mark of its love for God and the perseverance that He gives it in opposing its evil inclinations.

The greatest saints have been subjected to this trial (St. Paul among others) and yet they loved God very much. Our divine Savior, the Saint of saints, suffered Himself to be tempted for our instruction. That which He willed to bear in His sacred humanity could be neither a sin nor even an imperfection, for He was as incapable of the one as of the other. We cannot then be guilty when we suffer it as He did, resisting it according to the measure of our strength.

CHAPTER 3

In Temptation We Must Have Recourse to God

God sometimes sensibly guides the soul in these storms by which it is agitated. We then buffet courageously the impetuous flood of our passions. The vivid sense of God's presence, and the desire of loving Him that we feel, animate us and inspire us with confidence. But sometimes He conceals Himself; He seems to sleep, as He did in the bark of the disciples when it was on the point of being submerged in the raging sea. On such occasions the soul is endangered by the excessive fear that seizes and paralyzes the heart.

And yet there is nothing to fear if you will only lift your eyes to heaven, from which succor must come, and if you make use of its assistance. When the disciples were in danger of perishing, they lost no time in useless lamentation; they did not, in childish fear, give up all care of the ship; they strove manfully with the storm, and, turning to their Master, they implored His help. Jesus seemed asleep (Matt. 8:24) and yet He directed, without their being aware of it, the means that they employed to escape shipwreck. So, too, God, concealed as He is from sight, is not the less attentive to what is passing in your heart. To you it seems that the next moment will bring the wreck, and yet you make headway against the storm.

The motives that inspire you, the feelings that animate you and prompt your actions almost without your perceiving it, the courage that, ever on the point of failing, is always reviving, the constancy with which you reject deceitful pleasures, the sinful pleasures offered by the enemy: from whom do they come?

From yourself? Weak as you are, is this resistance yours alone? Does it not come from Jesus Christ, who, without making Himself perceived, affords you His powerful support, according to His word that He would "not let you be tempted beyond your strength" (1 Cor. 10:13, RSV). Yes, when you think Him farthest off, Jesus is in your heart. You think yourself forgotten, but you are more than ever present to His memory because you are in need. He is present at your combats as He was at that of St. Stephen (Acts 7:55) and, provided you do not lose confidence, He will make you victorious over your enemies by preserving you from consenting to their wicked designs.

CHAPTER 4

How to Recognize Whether We Have Consented to Temptation

We have not much difficulty in seeing that temptation is no evil and that consent alone makes the sin. That which troubles and disquiets those whom God subjects to this painful trial is the fear of offending God and their ignorance of the principles by which they may reassure themselves, not being able to distinguish between temptation and consenting to temptation.

This uncertainty as to their consent fills them with an anxiety, which causes them great suffering, destroys their interior peace, and so weakens their confidence as to prevent them from approaching God freely and with confidence, and, in fine, throws them into extreme despondency, utterly prostrating their strength. A few reflections would suffice to clear their doubts and enable them to come to a right decision.

We have not a complete command over our mind and our heart. We cannot wholly prevent the intrusions of certain thoughts and feelings. Sometimes indeed they take such forcible possession of us that without perceiving it, we are led to pursue in spirit the thought or design that thus presents itself. Our preoccupation is so great that we hear and see nothing of what is passing around; we do not even remember how or when these thoughts or feelings commenced. Thus, we often suddenly find ourselves, to our surprise, engaged in thoughts and feelings that are opposed to charity or to other virtues, or in projects of vanity, pride, or self-love.

This state continues a longer or a shorter time according to the strength of the imagination or the sensible impression that occasioned it, or until some circumstance arises to awaken our soul from this apparent enchantment. We then perceive, by reflection, the nature of our thoughts.

If in this moment of self-consciousness, we condemn the thought or feeling, if we disavow it and strive to reject it, we may safely say that in all that went before we were not to blame. The satisfaction that we experience in being freed from it is a fresh proof that our will had no part in our reverie. In this preoccupation there was no deliberation, no choice on the part of the will.

In order to offend God it is necessary that the will should deliberately consent to something sinful that it is free to reject. In the case we have supposed, there was neither freedom nor deliberation; hence there could be no sin.

Moreover, the promptness of their rejection, when consciousness returned, showed the good dispositions of the soul and that it would not have admitted these thoughts and feelings, still less have dwelt on them, had reflection furnished the opportunity of accepting or rejecting them at will.

We must then consider these temptations as beginning only when we became conscious of their presence. It is to this moment, therefore, that our examination must be directed, and if we rejected them at that time, we may be at peace.

This abstraction may continue for a long time, as often happens at prayer, where we are carried away by distractions that entirely absorb the soul. This circumstance does not make it voluntary or deliberate. It no more depends on our will to shorten the distraction then, than it does to prevent it from coming at all; there is no more choice in the one than in the other. There will be no more sin either, for as the preoccupation that comes unforeseen is blameless, so the length of time in which it remains unperceived cannot make it culpable. There should be no difficulty, therefore, in deciding these cases.

CHAPTER 5

Short, Passing Temptations

Temptations are generally perceived at once or soon after they present themselves and may differ in kind. Sometimes they are thoughts or feelings that arise suddenly and pass away as quickly. In such a case, we are sometimes at a loss to determine whether it was merely a temptation or whether there was sin. Its duration was so short that although we turned away from it, we are unable to decide whether it was quickly enough to prevent consent.

In such circumstances, we may base our decision on our ordinary sentiments and conduct. If we esteem, love, and zealously practice the virtues against which these temptations are directed; if in our habitual disposition we are free from any voluntary sin against these virtues; if, in longer and more sustained temptations of the kind, we have been victorious in the struggle, we may prudently judge that those fleeting thoughts and feelings were merely temptations and not sins; and that the rejection that banished them had really forestalled consent.

The reason is that when we act contrary to our habitual disposition, we must use a certain violence that we cannot but perceive. If, then, we are habitually such as I have supposed, our consent to the temptation would not be a matter of ignorance or of doubt. The impression that such a consent would have made, although but passing, would have caused itself to be felt.

We may reassure ourselves, then, from the very fact that we are not certain of having yielded to the temptation. Our doubt itself proves that we may be certain, for had we really consented, we would not doubt.

All those who prescribe rules for persons who are troubled by temptations are unanimous in advising them to despise these passing thoughts and to pay as little attention to them as possible. The reason that they give is the result of experience, which teaches us that if we neglect them and pass them by in occupying ourselves with other things, they leave no impression and return less frequently or not at all; but, on the contrary, that if we attack them violently, if we subject them to a strict examination, and especially if we allow them to frighten us, we are only recalling what is already gone; we stop them and give them strength in the pause that we force them to make in our mind. That which, had we despised it, would have been but as a passing shadow or a fleeting gleam of lightning becomes by the attention we give it a devouring flame in our heart. It becomes an entrenched enemy, obstinate in the combat and dangerous to the soul.

Temptation is like a coward who seeks to test his adversary. If he meets with undisguised contempt or firm resistance, he does not push the quarrel, but retires. But if he encounters timid compromise or cowardly fear, he takes advantage of the weakness, attacks with violence, and obliges his enemy to submit to his terms.

We must, then, allow all such temptations to pass lightly by and reserve our attention for useful objects. If, when these thoughts arise, we simply turn our heart to God in some aspiration of love and piety, they will be unable to do us any harm.

CHAPTER 6

Persistent, Troublesome Temptations

Ordinarily, temptations are not so easily vanquished and their attack is strong and continued. If they cease for a while, it is only to return to the charge. And as they agitate both mind and heart, a timid soul is apt to fear a sin in feelings that we so frequently experience and that seem to maintain a fixed dwelling in the heart.

The fear thus excited increases the feeling; the agitation in which the soul finds itself and the failure of its efforts to overcome the trouble give rise to a despondency more dangerous than the temptation itself, since it takes away the strength that is required for successful resistance.

Our conduct during the presence of the temptation may serve to determine whether we are deserving of blame. And in the first place, to prevent ourselves from being overcome by doubts that are dangerous and unreasonable, we should return to the principles that we first established.

The feeling that is experienced in the moment of temptation is not in itself a voluntary consent. It is only the bait with which the enemy hopes to gain the consent. He presents the object to the mind or fancy; that is a thought. He renders it pleasing to the desires or passions; that is a feeling, which is the natural consequence of the representation of the object. This feeling is more or less vivid according to the temperament of the individual and the impression caused by the object. But all this is independent of the will and precedes the consent.

To produce the consent, it is necessary that the will should deliberately adhere to this feeling, that it should approve it, attach itself to it, and agree to it. An idea may dwell in the mind, a feeling may exist in the heart, without being adopted by the will. It is thus that we resist or reject the inspirations of the good spirit as well as those of the bad. This first thought, then, or feeling, which only proposes an object to our will, no more constitutes a sin than it does a virtue, since these both consist in the choice that is made by the will in finally attaching itself to either.

If, then, the soul, in the time of temptation, had recourse to God for the grace of which it stood in need; if it renounced the feeling that was opposed to virtue; if it disapproved and rejected it and abhorred all that the temptation proposed; if it sought to turn away the thought by fixing the mind on some proper or useful object; then, even though it cannot answer with certainty for its fidelity during each instant of the continuance of the trial, it may safely judge that all that it experienced, no matter how violent it appeared to be or how long continued, was simply and merely a temptation in which there was no fault.

God does not permit the soul to be tempted beyond its strength, as the Holy Spirit teaches us: "God is faithful, and he will not let you be tempted beyond your strength, but with the temptation will also provide the way of escape, that you may be able to endure it" (1 Cor. 10:13, RSV). He is never wanting to the one who does all he can to avoid sin. And it is certain that when we employ the means that religion and

experience point out, we cannot reproach ourselves
with negligence. We must then encourage the hope
that He who in His mercy gave us the fidelity to use
the proper means has also, according to His promise,
preserved us from falling. This reasoning must silence
the anxious doubts and fears that may arise when God
has caused the calm to succeed the storm.

The temptation may be strong enough to excite
bad impressions on our senses. They should not alarm
us. What we have said of feelings or sentiments is
equally applicable to impressions or sensations. Sensible impressions do not depend on the will, which,
not having the power to stop or to banish them, is not
responsible for their commencement or their persis-
tence. In such circumstances, there is no sin save in
their approval or acceptance. So long as we regard
them as the consequence of a temptation that we combat and condemn, we do not approve them and are
not to blame.

These impressions or sensations would only increase if we were to attend to them and vainly strive to
banish them. Since they are not sins, we must not allow them to trouble us. Our attention must be directed

solely to driving away from the mind and the heart the temptation that causes them and to guarding against the consent that it solicits.

CHAPTER 7

Temptations That Disturb Us in the Exercise of Virtues

All these principles will serve to sustain and encourage the soul in certain temptations that are experienced in the exercise of virtue. There are persons to whom the enemy does not dare to propose the abandonment of those virtues that lead to perfection; but he makes use of artifice to restrain them and to fix them in a mediocrity that degenerates into negligence. When they are not engaged in spiritual exercises, he leaves them alone, but no sooner do they apply themselves to these than he fills their imagination with a thousand ideas that disturb them.

In those who aspire to lead a life of perfection, without being deterred therefrom either by human respect or by the fear of the sacrifices that it entails, he inspires a secret pride in the fulfillment of their duties. This thought insinuates itself into all their occupations. It seems to them as though in everything they sought the vain esteem of men or their own self-satisfaction.

These temptations are so powerful in some as to discourage and altogether disconcert them. Possessed with the idea that on account of a want of purity of intention all their sacrifice is without fruit and without reward, they prefer to resist the inspirations of heaven; they interrupt their exercises of piety and lead a life filled with imperfections and with faults. Through a dread of the struggle in which they must engage, they omit the good works that God inspires, and thus, in avoiding one snare, they fall into another.

If the temptation arises from useless occupations in which we engage, or from dangerous occasions not required by our state of life, there can be no doubt that we should abandon them in order to secure ourselves; but, on the other hand, it is equally certain that we must not, through fear of temptation, fail to perform our duty and follow the guidance of the Spirit of God.

Temptation is not of itself an evil, whereas it is surely an evil to be wanting in our duty in that which God requires. If we allow ourselves to be influenced by this fear and on that account abandon our exercises of piety or the profit that attends a spirit of sacrifice, we are wanting in fidelity to grace; we deprive ourselves of the assistance that would enable us to advance in perfection; we place in the hand of our enemy a certain means of causing us to abandon successively all that we are bound to perform.

He will take advantage of this empire that he is allowed to acquire, of this fear that he has succeeded in inspiring, and will lead us by degrees to the neglect of the practices of religion, of the sacraments, of all that nourishes piety.

Will a soul in such a state, without strength, without courage, afraid to seek in prayer and mortification the means of support, be able to resist successfully the assault of its enemy?

Let us not then fear such temptations, since, as we have often said, the fault is not in them, but in our consenting to the evil that they propose. Those that are more enduring we must encounter with confidence and love of God. Those that are but passing thoughts, no matter how frequent, we must despise and forget, renewing our intention of doing the will of God in all our actions. Then such temptations will bring with them no imperfections; they will even do us good, since they will cause a more frequent purifying of our intention. Thus shall good come from evil, and from a snare designed for our destruction we shall derive a means for our sanctification.

CHAPTER 8

Temptations Not to Be Reasoned With

There are certain passions that we can vanquish only by a direct attack — that is, by doing the reverse of what they suggest. Those that form the leading points of an unsubdued nature are of this number. Those who are subject to vanity, anger, susceptibility, quick and strong prejudices can surmount these passions only by practicing on occasion the virtues that are directly opposed to them.

They must not be satisfied with renouncing the feelings that those passions inspire, but they must mortify them by producing the opposite sentiments. If they seek only to avoid the occasions of their faults, they will not succeed in destroying the passion, and when they can no longer avoid the occasion, they will be almost certain to fall. It is by practicing humility and meekness, by self-renunciation, and by attentions to those against whom we have a prejudice that we give to those passions efficacious blows and ensure their defeat and the complete victory of him who is faithful in resisting every attack.

On the other hand, nothing is more damaging than the conduct of certain persons in the time of temptation. They believe that they are guilty of a fault in case they fail to exhaust themselves in reasoning down the suggestions of the temptation. They enter into a discussion with the passion that attacks them and that is never without a specious reason for its justification. They engage in a combat that is long and doubtful, and that need not have lasted a minute if they had refused to argue with their wily enemy or at least would have given them much less trouble to surmount.

This is especially the case in temptations against faith and hope, or in sentiments opposed to charity. They wish to assure themselves of their interior dispositions by going directly against the temptation, and they only involve themselves in trouble, doubts, and perplexities, and uselessly expose themselves to peril.

As soon as we reason with the temptation, particularly in difficult matters or where difficulties are easily excited and hard to answer for those who are not well informed in such matters, or in things that appeal to self-love, and that our natural malice approves, we are in the greatest danger of defeat. So it was that Eve fell.

Temptations that enter the soul through the senses and that offer a satisfaction that is in conformity with nature cause a very strong impression. That which we oppose to it, not being appreciable to the senses or affecting our nature, makes much less impression unless, indeed, it be strengthened by a very vivid faith. In the midst of our trouble, faith has frequently a difficulty in making itself heard, and our resistance to the passion becomes very weak.

Besides, in this sort of defense, the attention we give to the temptation keeps it alive and makes it more felt, so that every instant it seems to us that we have yielded our consent to its suggestions, and we become so troubled and dismayed as to be unable afterward to give a satisfactory account of our conduct.

In all such temptations, there is no surer way of defending ourselves than simply to banish the thought by occupying our minds with some pious sentiment. If thoughts can intrude themselves without the consent of the will, the will, on the other hand, can indirectly expel them by obliging the mind to occupy itself with other objects.

Nor is it necessary to select for this purpose such as are opposed to the temptation that assails us, it being sufficient to disavow or reject it by entertaining any thought or any act of virtue that may distract our attention, selecting in preference those that are to us most familiar or most striking.

Some, easily moved by the sufferings of the God become man for our sake, place themselves at the foot of the Cross of Jesus Christ, who, by the sacrifice of His life, expiated our sins. There they conceive a new sorrow for their faults and omissions and a new horror for whatever might crucify again in their hearts their dear Lord and Master.

Others, in imagination, fly for refuge within the Sacred Heart of Jesus, imploring His mercy and protection, and by penetrating into His goodness and compassion for them, excite within themselves a gratitude and a confidence that ensure their fidelity. These, moved especially by the love displayed by Jesus in giving Himself to them in the Holy Eucharist, make use of the sentiments inspired by His infinite mercy to withdraw their heart from everything that might offend so good a Lord.

Those imagining themselves at the moment in which they will be called upon to render an account to God dwell upon the thought of heaven and hell. They ask themselves, "If I were just about to appear before the tribunal of Jesus Christ, how should I then wish to have acted?" Occupying themselves earnestly with these objects so interesting to the Christian and so capable of withdrawing man from sin, penetrated with truths at once so touching, so striking, their hearts become insensible to the temptation, and their minds cease to entertain the thought.

There are few temptations that can persist long in the soul who, refusing to listen to or discuss the imaginary reasons of passion and animated by a lively confidence, turns to God in loving trust and implores His help through the intercession of the Blessed Virgin. This exercise of love for God, during the continuance of the temptation, is the best safeguard of the heart. It can never be overcome so long as it sustains this sentiment. To render it stronger and more enduring, the mind should recall the motives that are apt to nourish and increase it; the enemy will soon retire in confusion. A renewal of the attack should be met with the same defense.

It is desirable next to banish entirely from the mind and the heart the ideas and feelings that beget the danger. We shall do it most readily and surely by engaging ourselves in some other thoughts or occupations.

Indeed, there are occasions, especially when the temptation is unusually strong and obstinate, when it is desirable to take up some entertaining author, to engage in some bodily exercise, or to occupy ourselves earnestly in business or the discharge of our household duties. Such occupations fix the attention and free the mind from the seductive pictures of the imagination. When peace and calm have returned, the mind and heart will be more at liberty to think of God and to attach themselves to Him more closely.

A capital point in these combats is not allowing ourselves to be troubled or to relax our confidence, and especially to resist the very first attack. When we are disturbed by fear, we know not where to turn for assistance, being, in a manner, struck with blindness.

We do not think of seeking assistance; the heart knows not on what to resolve, since the intellect presents nothing to prompt its action.

We may verify this in our daily experience, as well in temporal as in spiritual things. How often have we not beheld a man in sudden danger, palsied by fear, lose his presence of mind; in vain is a help tendered to him, he cannot see it; he has safety at hand, and in seeking it, he turns his back upon it.

Show a bold front to the enemy, and you can then take surer measures to parry his blows; you will more readily perceive the means of conquering; and being more at ease, you will employ them with greater confidence.

And, once more, what cause is there for fear?

The devil can indeed suggest the most horrible sins, but can he oblige you to consent to them? That depends on your will, not on his. Why then be frightened at a result that lies completely at your own disposal? Why fear a consent that, with the assured assistance of grace you can certainly refuse? Stand firm, and you have nothing to fear from an enemy who can conquer only by your permission.

This courage will spring from your confidence in God, which you must be careful to sustain. When one is discouraged in temptation, he is already half overcome. His efforts are feeble because they are unsupported by those graces that confidence attracts. How could they be granted when, through fear, there is no thought of imploring them? He no longer considers the goodness and power of a God who is able and willing to defend His child.

And yet were he to ask with trusting faith, that power and goodness would be soon made manifest. The confidence of the royal psalmist should be his: "I will call upon the Lord; and I shall be saved from my enemies" (Ps. 17:4 [RSV = Ps. 18:3]).

"But," you may say, "how often have I not experienced my weakness in this temptation?"

Yes, because you have always been wanting in confidence. Be firm then, and you will never fall. St. Peter, walking on the waters at the command of Jesus Christ, began to sink as soon as he commenced to doubt; he was saved only by a return to confidence, which gained for him the protection of his divine Master.

In temptations, especially in those that are generally violent, be on your guard at the first attack and try to repress its first motions. If, by a feeble defense, you allow the imagination to become excited and the heart to be occupied, your negligence will serve to increase your weakness. A passion that is trifled with soon gains the upper hand. It was only a spark, easily extinguished; it becomes a flame that consumes all the faculties of the soul.

This advice is the more necessary in those temptations that are increased in violence by the impression they make on the senses. A special mercy is then required to preserve us unharmed amid the flames. Diligence in meeting the danger would either have preserved you from the temptation or would have assured you the protection of God, whereby you would have escaped without a wound.

When anything occurs that is strange to our experience, we should at once consult our confessor and make known to him the new temptation. He will teach us what means we must employ to resist and banish the adversary. This act of humility and Christian simplicity draws down special graces from heaven. Our Lord takes a special interest in the troubles of those who, according to the order of divine providence, seek to walk in the paths of obedience. It often happens that such temptations never attack us a second time, when revealed at once to the minister of God. If we conceal them in the hope that they will disappear, they gain time to fortify themselves and become more difficult to overcome.

CHAPTER 9

Frequent Temptations

When we are subject to frequent temptations, we must employ the intervals of attack in preparing ourselves and in gathering strength to resist. He who would make himself ready only when assailed is easily surprised and readily defeated. "In time of peace, prepare for war" is a well-known maxim. We should not neglect its warning in our spiritual combats, in which defeat is so much more important than in temporal affairs, since thereby we are deprived of an eternal kingdom.

This preparation consists in leading a life of recollection. When we are leading a happy and distracted life, we do not pay proper attention to what is passing in our heart. Temptations advance very far before we find ourselves roused to a sense of danger. The mind, being occupied with light and trifling things, finds difficulty in reflecting seriously on the motives that religion offers to counteract the solicitations of passion. But in interior recollection, occupied with God and holy things, we see the enemy from afar; we use the proper precautions, and we find in our habitual thoughts and feelings sufficient weapons for a successful defense. The mind occupied with the truths of faith and the heart habitually attached to virtue are not so easily shaken by the false allurements of passion.

The torch of faith reveals the depth of the precipice to which the temptation leads, and, filled with horror, we withdraw from the slippery descent. Assiduous prayer and the invocation of the saints, particularly of the Mother of God, open to us the treasures of heaven and procure for us those chosen graces for which the dissipated soul does not even think of asking.

If this recollected life is accompanied by a careful frequentation of the sacraments, we shall be still more secure. And even though we sometimes yield to temptation, we should not therefore withdraw from the sacraments but, on the contrary, should approach them more frequently. The sacrament of Penance was established not only for the remission of actual sins but also for conferring graces that may withhold us from others that we might commit and fortify us against the passions that lead us into sin.

In abstaining from the sacraments, then, we deprive ourselves of these graces and diminish our capacity for resistance. The more frequently we approach the sacrament of Penance, the greater is the horror that we conceive for sin. This horror, frequently renewed, becomes more rooted in the soul, more vivid in its effects, and fortifies it more powerfully in the moment of danger. Moreover, all the theologians unite in saying that when a person who is very much inclined to mortal sin has had the misfortune to fall, he should lose no time in being reconciled, since, being separated from God and deprived of sanctifying grace, he remains in the greatest danger of committing the sin again, on a recurrence of the temptation. It is therefore very prejudicial to delay having recourse to the sacrament of Penance, and still more so to abandon it altogether, or for a time.

Holy Communion, when we approach it after suitable preparation, is also a very powerful aid against temptation. We receive Jesus Christ, the Savior of souls, and after He has given Himself to us, can we believe that He will refuse the graces that are necessary to preserve us in union with Him? If He enters our heart, is it not that He may confirm it in virtue? The Holy Council of Trent, speaking of the Holy Eucharist, says: "Jesus Christ desired that this Sacrament should be received as the spiritual food of souls, that it should nourish and strengthen them ... and should be an antidote by which we should be delivered from our daily faults and preserved from mortal sins" (session 13, chap. 2).

If there is any time in which we have pressing need of help to confirm us in virtue, to strengthen us against the enemy of salvation, to preserve us from mortal sin, it is certainly when we are the object of frequent temptations. The celestial food, the powerful antidote, is never more needed. To deprive ourselves voluntarily of that assistance provided for such emergencies would be to court peril and tempt our weakness.

Besides, when preparing ourselves for the Blessed Sacrament, we are absorbed in the thoughts suggested by the great event; our heart, occupied by the sentiments of piety that it strives to excite, recoils from temptation and is attentive to exclude everything that may diminish the graces that it solicits. But of this point the confessor is the proper judge; it is for him to prescribe what is to be done, lest in this we should be guided by illusions.

To all these safeguards against the temptations to which we are exposed, we may add the exercise of penance. It obtains new graces; it humbles the spirit; it deadens the passions; it expiates our sins, our faults, and our negligences; it excites our fervor and redoubles our vigilance. In this, however, there is need of discretion and judgment.

We must not carry our mortification too far, for then it would be an excess and prejudicial to our health, which Christian prudence commands us to preserve. The practice of mortification is beneficial against nearly all the passions, but there are temptations in which it may be hurtful to some persons, according to their character and temperament. To such, mortification must be forbidden, and they must do nothing of the kind, save by counsel and permission.

CHAPTER 10

The Utility of
Temptations

If temptations render us so unhappy, it is because we do not look upon them from the right point of view. We consider only the danger to which we are exposed, the evil to which we are drawn; we lose sight of the advantages that they confer, of the spiritual benefit that they can procure. This ignorance, or this want of reflection, accounts for the little profit that we derive from these trials. The following considerations will serve to make us bear them more patiently and will give us greater facility in overcoming them.

Temptations may be made to lead a Christian heart to the practice of the most solid virtues and to the acquisition of great merits in heaven. It is a great consolation to think that we can derive advantages from the very enemies that assail us and make them contribute to our happiness. Surely this thought should animate us in the hour of combat. It is the motive proposed to us by the apostle St. James: "Esteem it, my brethren, all joy, when you shall fall into diverse temptations," and he at once assigns the reason, "knowing that the trying of your faith worketh patience" and, he adds, "patience worketh perfection" (cf. James 1:2–4).

Man does not sufficiently reflect on himself; he does not know himself; he avoids self-examination lest perchance he should recognize faults that would cause him to blush. All his attention is engaged in endeavoring to excuse his sins to himself and to exaggerate his good qualities. From this foolish conduct springs that self-love so delicate, so sensitive, so touchy; that self-esteem and presumption that expose him to so many dangers; that vanity, that preference that he gives himself over others. Pride, the source of all evils, blinds him to his defects, to his falls, and to his weakness.

Even pious persons are not exempt from this self-complacency, this dwelling on one's virtues, this hunger for esteem, which are so natural to man. It is a secret spring of pride and vanity, which exalts them in their own eyes, puffs them up with satisfaction, leads them to rely on their own strength, and keeps them in a rash and dangerous feeling of security. It is a subtle poison that infects actions that are, in appearance, most holy.

Temptations are a sovereign remedy against this dangerous evil and its pernicious consequences. They reveal to man the interior of his own heart; they show him what he is when left to himself; they tear away all concealment and all disguise. By the light of their gloomy torch he sees his misery, his weakness, his corruption. Attacked alternately by the different passions, by envy, jealousy, hatred, vengeance, and by others, lower yet and more degrading, he sees in his heart the germs of all those disorders into which others have fallen and he is at last persuaded that his nature is not superior to theirs.

The first effect produced in us by such a sight is to inspire a humility proportioned to the misery that is thereby made known to us, where there is subject only for humility and contempt. The complacency that we might feel at the sight of certain good qualities that we possess is soon lowered by that crowd of evil inclinations against which we must wage unceasing warfare.

We see ourselves such as we should appear to men were our heart with all its passions unveiled to their contemplation. We feel for ourselves a Christian contempt, humility before God, and at least equality with other men.

What advantages could we not derive from this self-knowledge accompanied by the spirit of religion? If we are suffering submissive to the designs of providence, we acknowledge that God is lenient toward us and does not treat us as the corruption of our heart deserves. If we are happy and consoled, we adore the goodness of God, who is so indulgent to His unworthy creature. The contrast of our unworthiness and the divine goodness excites the liveliest gratitude and inspires a more perfect love. With the conviction that we are unworthy of the benefits that we receive at His hands and that flow from His infinite mercy, we strive to deepen still more our humility, that virtue at once so necessary and the mother of so many other virtues.

One to whom temptations have revealed all the corruption of his heart experiences, alone with God, the same confusion that he would suffer before men to whom it should be known. It is a salutary confusion that should be preserved.

Hereafter, guided by the spirit of religion, he will not be irritated by the conduct of others, rough and disagreeable though it be. The light of faith shows him that he merits even more contempt than he receives, and if he does not meet with more, it is because he is not thoroughly known to others, or their charity blinds them to that which they might otherwise perceive. Is anything more needed to destroy forever his self-complacency and esteem?

CHAPTER 11

Attachment to God and
the Exercise of Vigilance

The knowledge that temptations give of the interior produces another effect that, rightly followed up, leads to perfection. One who is subject to temptations and yet desirous of being saved attaches himself more closely to God and is excited to greater vigilance over himself — two great means of advancing rapidly in the path of sanctity.

He sees in his heart a number of enemies; he knows his own weakness; and although he feels that with ordinary grace he has sufficient resolution to overcome some, yet against others to which he is more violently drawn and in certain occasions of greater peril, he is convinced from his own weakness, from a sorrowful experience, and from a knowledge of the principles of his religion, that without special graces, he will not have the courage to resist successfully.

Knowing these things and alarmed at the unequal struggle, what is he to do? He must seek help powerful enough to sustain him against his enemies and particularly against those whom he most fears. Faith teaches him that this assistance is to be found only in God, and that to obtain it he has only to implore it fervently and perseveringly. To Him then does he turn with entire confidence.

At the first movement of the temptation, he says with the psalmist, "I have lifted up my eyes to the mountains from whence help shall come to me" (Ps. 120:1 [RSV = Ps. 121:1]); he solicits it by his prayers; he attracts it by his desires; all the aspirations of his heart are eloquent to obtain it. The more the temptation presses him, the more he attaches himself to God. He is like a child walking along the edge of fearful precipices or surrounded by ferocious beasts of prey. He clings to his Father for protection whenever the path grows slippery and dangerous or when the fierce growl or the fiery eye warns him of mortal peril.

Under the protection of God, like the royal prophet, he ceases to fear enemies who are powerless against a strong faith pointing to eternal happiness and a firm hope that gains those special graces promised to implicit confidence. He no longer regards the enemy whom he had thought well-nigh invincible; he despises him or attacks him with confidence, and in such dispositions he meets with an easy victory. This grace, frequently renewed, teaches him all the more the extent of God's goodness and mercy in his regard, and in return his love grows fervent and strong.

Temptations then, properly understood and met according to the spirit of religion, attach us more closely to God by the great virtues of faith, hope, and charity, to the frequent exercise of which they oblige us.

On the other hand, the conviction of our weakness inevitably excites us to greater vigilance. A weak man is a timid man — timid in proportion to his weakness. That weakness makes him very careful not to make to himself enemies and to avoid the anger of those whom he has already made. He is attentive to his own behavior and weighs every word. Doubtful of his own strength, he seeks to attack no one.

This conduct is but a figure of the precaution that a Christian should take. He avoids with care whatever may excite the temptations to which he is subject, whatever may give rise to new and untried dangers. He knows who it is that says, "He that loveth danger shall perish in it" (Ecclus. 3:27 [RSV = Sir. 3:27]). In the fear of being left to his own weakness by rendering himself, through presumption, unworthy of the assistance of heaven, he is all attention to what passes in his mind and heart, lest some new enemy should creep in, or lest those already there concealed, taking advantage of his negligence, should take him by surprise, gain him with the poisoned sweetness of passion, and force him to the precipice.

Vigilance is the more necessary, because the temptation is not unfrequently disguised. It uses strategies; it alleges false pretexts; it takes upon itself the appearance of virtue so as to draw the soul quietly to the fatal trap. Passion often conceals itself, lest it should be recognized. It will insinuate itself insensibly into the heart and disguise itself so as to enter unperceived. He who is inattentive to its approach gives it time to fortify itself or fails to erect a barrier strong enough to resist its attack.

On the contrary, he who is exercised in the spiritual warfare and aware of the danger of new temptations or of giving the slightest way to the old, is always on the alert to detect the slightest movement of his heart. He examines the nature of his feelings and no sooner does he perceive the enemy than he challenges him and stands to his own defense.

And this vigilance is an assured bulwark against temptations, whether from without or from within. With it there can be no surprise, and the enemy finds the garrison prepared at all points.

In time of peace and calm, precaution is regarded as superfluous. But in time of war or in the midst of the tempest, we must be vigilant to escape shipwreck or defeat. And so it is that frequency of temptation begets vigilance, and vigilance causes a stricter union with God, and from this union springs docility to the inspirations of the Holy Spirit, and docility leads us in the path of perfection.

CHAPTER 12

The Good Effects of Temptation in Negligent Souls

Temptations, which seemed destined to be the certain ruin of negligent souls, have not unfrequently been a heaven-provided means of rescuing them from the tepidity in which they lived and of leading them to the fervent practice of virtue.

There are persons who live a life of languishing piety. No marked disorder is visible in their general conduct, but neither is there any endeavor after perfection. If they do not commit any of those mortal offenses that cut us off from God, neither do they do any great good, through their indifference to the mortification of the senses, their indulgence of every feeling and inclination not manifestly sinful, and their habitual disregard of the persistent principles of the Faith. Their lives, having so little of the supernatural, are but indifferently meritorious in the sight of God. They are vessels becalmed on their voyage to heaven.

Well, God sends a storm to break the idle calm. Temptation comes to awaken slumbering piety, and God, enlightening them as to their state, draws them kindly to Him by His grace. They see themselves on the eve of perils from which they shrink affrighted. They find themselves beset by enemies alternately employing charms and fears to seduce or to intimidate.

Religion then makes herself known in all her strength. Alarmed at the danger, these persons have recourse to God, in whom alone they can have confidence of a favorable issue to the combat. If the assaults are renewed, they think seriously and resolutely of employing all the means that faith can offer to escape the impending ruin.

Henceforth, earnest in prayer, by which they hope to obtain the required strength; united with God, to whom a lively sense of danger has recalled them; watchful over themselves, so as not to fall into the snares prepared for them, they act only from motives of piety and live in the continual exercise of virtue.

All that they desire, all that they do, is offered up as an act of homage to God. The more they are assailed by temptations, the more firmly do they determine to continue in the path that alone conducts to a place of safety. From a life of tepidity, they enter on a life of fervor in which every moment is consecrated to God.

This change necessarily takes place in us if we are faithful to grace. For, attacked by temptations, seeing our salvation at stake and wishing to avoid a loss that is irreparable, however slightly we may reason from the principles of faith, we cannot but recognize that it would be presumption, and a very sinful presumption, to expect, from the hands of God, a victory that we take no steps to ensure.

To live a tepid and dissipated life, to omit or negligently to perform our accustomed exercises of piety, to approach the sacraments rarely and with but little preparation, to be careless about the commission of venial sins, and yet to expect from the mercy of God the grace to resist our passions is only to tempt Him, to render ourselves unworthy of His assistance, to deserve that we should be abandoned to our own weakness and become the slave of sin.

With such dispositions, a tepid and negligent soul cannot be said with justice really to intend resistance; for to wish the end while we reject the means is not to wish at all. God must then say as He said to His chosen people: "Destruction is thy own, O Israel: thy help is only in me" (Hos. 13:9).

It is not of such that I treat, but rather of those who, in spite of their tepidity, fear sin and love God enough to shrink from a mortal offense and to adopt the means that are necessary for their preservation. To such souls, temptations are very useful, arousing them from their sloth and exciting their fervor.

Those who treat of the spiritual life teach us that God sometimes permits a tepid soul to fall into some grievous fault in order to rouse it from its lethargy by the remorse that follows sin.

CHAPTER 13

The Value of Time Spent in Overcoming Temptations

Some persons, much subject to temptations, lament the time they spend in resisting them. "I cannot," they say, "preserve recollection. When I try to meditate, to recite some prayers, to spend a few moments in the presence of the Blessed Sacrament, I cannot fix my mind on God. That is the very time that temptations come to assail me; and I pass it in a vain endeavor to banish them. I meet these troublesome and obstinate visitors even at the holy table, when I go to receive my Lord and my God. What profit can I expect from pious exercises performed in such a manner?"

This thought brings great discouragement. To cure this, to reassure and console such persons, it is important to recall to them the principles by which to correct their error and the advantages of such a state when borne as it should be.

It is a maxim universally acknowledged that we are not called to serve God according to our feelings and inclinations, but in the way that He requires and according to His goodwill. God attaches His graces and rewards not precisely to the good works that we prescribe for ourselves but to those that He authorizes and enjoins.

Based on this principle is the decision that, if obedience prescribes an employment that keeps us from prayer or meditation, by performing the action in a spirit of recollection, we please God just as much as if we had spent the time in communion with Him. And if we were to omit the action for the sake of praying or meditating, we would not be serving God as He requires; we would offend instead of serving Him.

This principle should suffice to convince you that you do not lose the time that you pass in resisting temptations that occur during your exercises of piety. The devil has no more power over men than God allows him. It was only by an express permission that he was enabled to subject the patient Job to so many trials and temptations. God permits this state in which you find yourself; and as distractions are a species of temptation, you must apply to them what I have just been saying.

How then does God wish that you should serve Him? Is it by a sustained and uninterrupted meditation on holy things? Is it by tender colloquies with Him that no earthly affection shall be allowed to disturb?

No. He wishes you to serve Him by a faithful and persevering resistance to all the inspirations of the enemy, by which he strives to seduce and separate you from the divine love; that, like the Jews rebuilding the walls of Jerusalem, one hand should grasp the sword of defensive warfare while the other labors to erect the spiritual edifice of perfection in a sentiment of lively faith and unshaken hope (Neh. 4:17) — a hope, I mean, unshaken in your will, however it may seem to waver in your imagination.

Has such been your fidelity?

Then you have done the will of God; you have honored Him as He required; you have put Him above everything else; you have in your submission and patience and fidelity in resisting temptation been as pleasing to Him as though you had been occupied in an ecstasy of fervent prayer distinguished by the most affectionate sentiments.

I ask you, how can that time be lost that is spent in conformity to the will of God and in the exhibition of so marked and solid an attachment to Him? After such an exercise, in which you have courageously resisted all the attacks of your enemies, you should be as well satisfied as if you had performed it in the greatest recollection and tranquillity. It had less savor and sweetness, but the fruit was all the richer.

You have done the will of God, and He will acknowledge it in the graces with which He will enrich your soul. The accomplishment of that will was painful; the pain will not be forgotten in the recompense. The Holy Spirit assures us by the mouth of the Apostle: "God is not unjust, that He should forget your work, and the love which you have shown in His name" (Heb. 6:10).

The time, therefore, so employed is not lost, not only because we render God the honor and service that He asks at our hands and in the very way He asks it, but also because in these combats we acquire merits that are being multiplied in every minute. Persecutions that increased the sufferings of the martyrs enriched their crown of triumph; temptations are a persecution that has the same effect in a faithful soul.

The Holy Spirit declares him blessed who "could have transgressed, and hath not transgressed; who could do evil things, and hath not done them" (Ecclus. 31:10 [RSV = Sir. 31:10]). His happiness is proportioned to the merit that he amassed by his perseverance.

On this principle, when you observe the law of God and do His will in a way that is displeasing to nature, you acquire a double claim to reward: first, you have obeyed, and secondly, you have obeyed with difficulty and against resistance and combat. The sacrifice you have made of the natural inclination that solicited and impelled you is rewarded here by new graces and hereafter by an increase of eternal glory and happiness.

Following up this reasoning, what an immense treasure of merit that person accumulates who, assailed by all kinds of temptations, is steadfast in clinging to God! He is certain that every sacrifice was noted: every one had its merit; every one shall have its recompense. On each separate occasion that he resisted temptation, it could be said of him, "Blessed is he, for he could have transgressed, and hath not transgressed; he could do evil things, and hath not done them."

And what a vast number of sacrifices are made by that one who, often drawn and urged by passion, constantly resists its seductions and refuses the object that it presents to his concupiscence. Few moments pass unmarked by victory. The repeated and varied assaults of the enemy serve only to swell the number of victims that the faithful warrior immolates to God. What a treasure of merits in these hand-to-hand struggles with passion!

We do not ourselves perceive every sacrifice that we make, but the all-seeing eye of God does not suffer one to escape. Is anything more needed to console us in this state and to encourage us to perseverance?

If the contest is severe, the crown is brilliant; one minute of pain and an eternity of glory! And who would wish to exchange eternal glory for a minute's gratification?

Nor is the merit restricted to these repeated sacrifices; new treasures are found in the interior virtues practiced at such a time. We feel very well that we cannot maintain successful resistance without the aid of heaven, without the light and the motives of faith, the inspirations of hope, and the support of divine charity. Our heart is occupied in a continual exercise of prayer and in forming repeated acts of these exalted virtues. If only one act of divine charity is so powerful as to reconcile a sinner with God, how much merit does he not acquire who in his combats is constantly repeating this act!

What ignorance, then, to suppose that time so employed in resisting temptation is lost for heaven and perfection, when, on the contrary, it is evident from what has been said that we are laboring most actively to practice the one and gain the other!

Sophia Institute

Sophia Institute is a nonprofit institution that seeks to nurture the spiritual, moral, and cultural life of souls and to spread the Gospel of Christ in conformity with the authentic teachings of the Roman Catholic Church.

Sophia Institute Press fulfills this mission by offering translations, reprints, and new publications that afford readers a rich source of the enduring wisdom of mankind.

Sophia Institute also operates two popular online Catholic resources: CrisisMagazine.com and CatholicExchange.com.

Crisis Magazine provides insightful cultural analysis that arms readers with the arguments necessary for navigating the ideological and theological minefields of the day. *Catholic Exchange* provides world news from a Catholic perspective as well as daily devotionals and articles that will help you to grow in holiness and live a life consistent with the teachings of the Church.

In 2013, Sophia Institute launched Sophia Institute for Teachers to renew and rebuild Catholic culture through service to Catholic education. With the goal of nurturing the spiritual, moral, and cultural life of souls, and an abiding respect for the role and work of teachers, we strive to provide materials and programs that are at once enlightening to the mind and ennobling to the heart; faithful and complete, as well as useful and practical.

Sophia Institute gratefully recognizes the Solidarity Association for preserving and encouraging the growth of our apostolate over the course of many years. Without their generous and timely support, this book would not be in your hands.

www.SophiaInstitute.com
www.CatholicExchange.com
www.CrisisMagazine.com
www.SophiaInstituteforTeachers.org

Sophia Institute Press® is a registered trademark of Sophia Institute. Sophia Institute is a tax-exempt institution as defined by the Internal Revenue Code, Section 501(c)(3). Tax I.D. 22-2548708.